Introducti

St. Paul wrote, "T
and peace" (Gala
joyful spirit we ne
above all, joy is a gift from God.

A truly joyful life is only possible when you clear your mind of all kinds of fear, resentment, hatred, and vindictiveness. It's a big order, but no one said it would be easy. Jesus said, "Do not be afraid."

The virtue of hope comes into play here. We hear the Lord speaking to us, "In this world you will have troubles," but "take heart (and be of good cheer) for I have overcome the world."

Joy is the simplest form of gratitude, and the greatest honor we can give to Almighty God. Be at peace, then, and try to live joyfully because of God's love.

My dear friends, I offer this little book as a personal gift of love. I want to help you to stop unintentionally sabotaging your chances for greater happiness and joy. By coping better with your fears and removing toxic thoughts from your mind, you will be able to feel God's joy pulsing though your soul, which is the most wonderful gift one can ever receive. I wish you every blessing.

May the Lord be your strength and your joy!
Father Jack Catoir

"Christ came to bring joy;
joy to parents, joy to children;
joy to teachers, joy to students;
joy to friends and families;
joy to the sick and elderly;
joy to all people.
Joy is indeed the
keynote message of Christianity,
and the recurring motif
of the Gospels.
Go therefore and become
messengers of joy."

POPE JOHN PAUL II

Second printing 2009

Twenty-Third Publications, A Division of Bayard, One Montauk Avenue, Suite 200, New London, CT 06320, (860) 437-3012 or (800) 321-0411, www.23rdpublications.com

ISBN 978-1-58595-714-9

Cover photo: ©iStockphoto.com/Christian Ardelean

Contents

1 The Secret of Happiness

Happiness is a butterfly
which when pursued is just out of grasp...
But if you will sit down quietly,
may alight upon you.

NATHANIEL HAWTHORNE

In 1953, I was walking guard duty at midnight on Christmas Eve. There I was, a lonely Army draftee serving at Fort Sam Houston in San Antonio, Texas. My civilian life seemed a million miles away. I could hear the choir singing at the post chapel, where Midnight Mass was being held, and I felt terribly lonely.

It never dawned on me that I was giving in to self-pity, and thereby was missing a wonderful opportunity to come closer to God. It would have been so much better had I united spiritually with the choir and thought of God as a friend who was closer to me than my own heartbeat.

If I had said, "Thank you, Lord, for being here with me," I might have felt his presence and been able to offer him my love in return. I wasn't at that stage yet. I didn't realize that joy never comes to those who are caught up in their own brooding.

Blessed Elizabeth of the Trinity, a 19th-century mystic, wrote, "The secret of happiness, and the secret of all the saints, is that they learned to love God as a friend." To love God as a friend is such a simple thing to say, but very few are able to do it.

The saints relate to God in a calm and intimate way. They stay focused on the God who loves saints and sinners alike. You don't have to be extra special to be God's friend. Jesus is a friend to all those who call upon him.

Never let your confidence in God's love be undermined by self-pity. Make a simple act of faith. Call on the Lord and accept his love. When you focus too much on your woes and worries instead of on God's wonderful mercy, that elusive butterfly of happiness that Hawthorne spoke about never descends. Learn to live joyfully because of the knowledge of God's love. It may take a little effort in the beginning, but in time it becomes easier.

Rising to a higher level of joy is simply a matter of changing your thinking pattern. The thoughts you think soon become the emotions you feel. If you think you're alone in the world, your feelings of loneliness will intensify. But you are never alone. Your best friend, the King of kings, is always with you.

Dear Lord, you are my friend, I believe it
and I trust you with my life.

2 Grace Is Amazing

Back in 1977, I learned that a Catholic multimedia organization called The Christophers was searching for a new director. I had been an admirer of their founder, Father James Keller, ever since I was a teenager.

Communications was the mission of this New York City-based media organization, which included a radio and television-production company and a publishing house that produced spiritual books and pamphlets.

To get that job would be a dream come true because of my college ambition to get into television production, but I knew I didn't have a chance. Working as a Catholic priest in various parishes for the previous 17 years, and being in charge of the Marriage Tribunal of the Diocese of Paterson for 10 years, hardly had given me the media experience they needed.

I thought, *Why even bother to apply?* sabotaging my chances from the outset. Also, I didn't feel worthy of being Father Keller's successor. This negativity killed my initial enthusiasm. For three weeks I did nothing, until one morning a burst of energy hit me. I suddenly thought, *What have I got to lose?*

Immediately I wrote a letter applying for the position. This avalanche of courage took over before I had a chance to question it any further.

Looking back, I now see that it was a grace from

God. Actual grace is defined as a light to the mind and an impulse to the will. God influences us without taking our freedom away. Once I realized that the only thing holding me back from applying was my fear of being rejected, I jumped at the opportunity.

Through God's grace, I was given new purpose and direction. I see now that it's very important to see the connection between God's grace and our own private lives. Fear and insecurity cannot be allowed to prevail, not ever.

Theology becomes a living reality when we understand that grace is a personal gift from God, helping us to be happy and productive.

A year after I applied for the job, and many interviews later, the board of directors chose me to be the new director. I was both flabbergasted and jubilant.

Isn't God's grace amazing?

For the next 18 years I did radio and television shows, wrote books and articles, and gave talks around the world, bringing the Christopher message to millions of people. One of the themes of our programs was this: "There is no one like you, and you can make a difference." God is always acting in our lives; sometimes subtly, and sometimes in dramatic ways.

Dear Lord, help me to have the courage to follow my dreams. Thank you for being there to help me.

3 Fear Is the Enemy of Joy

The fear of failure dominates the thinking of many people. People tend to become perfectionists in order to avoid failing. This nervous condition can lead to self-sabotage in a thousand ways. But isn't it true that nobody can be perfect? We all have to live with our imperfections and still love ourselves in the process.

I knew a 40-year-old woman who quit college years earlier because she was afraid of failing her first set of exams. Instead of trusting herself to pass the exams, she just didn't show up. In fact she dropped out of school entirely. This type of fear caused her problems throughout her entire life. She didn't know how to cope and didn't have faith enough to trust her fears to the Lord.

Faith brings with it a new confidence. Once you know that you are loved, good things begin to happen. Faith teaches us that God loves us; and God gives us the grace we need to succeed. Patience and trust are the keys to a peaceful life. There is no need to be afraid.

The words "do not be afraid" are repeated 365 times in the Bible. They are words of wisdom coming directly from God. Once we believe them and act on them, we can become more secure and peaceful.

There are many kinds of fear. For instance, jealousy and envy are forms of fear. Jealousy is the worry that someone is taking what is rightfully yours. Envy is fear that you are not getting your fair share because of the good fortune of another.

The fear of failing goes to the heart of all our fears. We don't want to lose what we perceive to be necessary for our happiness.

But think about it. Do you really need what you think you need? Or do you merely think you need it?

How sad it is to fear losing something that you don't really need. Think it through! Let go of the fears that weigh you down.

Making progress may take time, but your patience and trust in the Lord will carry you through. Prayer will put you in touch with God's power. Ask for the gift of a true faith, and God will eventually do for you what you cannot yet do for yourself.

Once you build up a solid level of trust in God, your soul will soar.

Here is a prayer written by St. Teresa of Avila. It may help you along the way:

> *Dear Lord, let nothing disturb me, let nothing cause me fear. Teach me that trust and patience obtains all.*

4 God Delights in You

A new grandmother couldn't wait to hold her infant grandson. She was ecstatic over his birth. She snuggled him, kissed him, and thanked God over and over for giving the family such a marvelous gift. Her love for him was pure joy.

Love and joy are always two sides of the same coin.

Did you ever stop to think that God feels the same way about you as this grandmother felt about her grandchild? Isn't it true that when you love someone, you delight in loving him or her?

No one loves in an abstract way. The love fills you with joy.

As difficult as it may be to believe, the fact is that God not only loves you, God delights in loving you.

"God will exult with joy over you…he will renew you by his love."

The lover always enjoys being with his beloved. Joy is based in the very nature of love. "God so loved the world that he gave his only Son so that everyone who believes in him…may have eternal life" (John 3:16). This statement is more than a theological concept; it is also a psychological fact.

Out of love for us, Jesus died on a cross. Just as the grain of wheat falls to the ground and dies so that new life can begin, so did Jesus give up his life that we might awaken to a new and higher life of love and joy.

The grandmother would gladly give her life to save the life of her new grandchild. She would be glad to give and not count the cost. That's what true love does.

Jesus Christ wants to share his infinite love with us. "Whoever seeks to gain his life will lose it, but whoever loses his life will preserve it" (Luke 17:33). This tells us of the selflessness that comes from true love.

God wants to be with us. God's deep yearning for us is eternal. Once we understand this and believe it, we can cast away our doubts. The next step is to beg for his mercy and put on the indomitable will to count our blessings.

In spite of our unworthiness, we need to believe that God is infinitely more than a doting grandmother. Accept the Lord's unchanging love and be at peace.

Dear Lord, I bow before the wonder of your love, and I thank you.

5 Make Room for Trust

A 40-year-old diabetic named Paul lost his job and went into a funk. He had serious health issues and was running out of cash. He tried prayer but felt God was not listening.

By sheer accident, he came across a quote from Pope John Paul II. Ordinarily it would have passed right by him, but it must have been a grace, because he was stopped in his tracks when he read these words: "Christianity is about salvation that comes from a loving God."

That thought touched him deeply. The idea that we are all being prepared for eternal life according to God's plan made him ponder the deeper mystery of life. He felt called to trust God more, but didn't know how to go about it. He needed a path out of the fear and self-pity that were tearing him apart.

He took a deep breath and accepted in blind faith that the Lord's love was guiding his life. He didn't understand it, but he began to see that the beautiful saving plan of God sometimes leads us down paths we would not have chosen for ourselves.

Faith enables us to see the miracle of God's love present at every stage of life, and joy is the simplest response to God's love and beauty. For this reason he took to heart these words of St. Paul, the patron saint he was named after, but hardly ever thought about, "Rejoice always, in all circumstances give thanks to the Lord."

The frustrated man decided to trust God more. He began to focus on the beauty of creation all around him, and he suspended fear about the future. It wasn't easy, but trusting that God would help him find his way made a big difference in his emotional life. He persevered in his good intentions and developed a good frame of mind, which in turn helped him to find a new job. It paid less, but he was happy. Then he met a lovely young woman, became friends with her, and his whole perspective changed.

Attaining spiritual joy may seem "impossible for mortals, but with God all things are possible" (Luke 18:27).

Here was a man who, just weeks before, thought he was at the end of his rope. When his attitude changed, his life improved immensely. An amazing grace had been given to him to trust God more, and to expect the best.

We all have to do a better job of trusting the past to God's mercy and the future to God's Divine Providence.

Lord, give me the grace I need to trust you more and more. Yes, I believe, but help me in my unbelief.

6 Passing on the Faith

"We are an Easter people," said St. Augustine, "and Alleluia is our song." But there are many good Christians who never feel very joyful. Let me tell you about two nuns who were teaching in the same school. I knew them personally, and they were both good women. However, one was stern and humorless; the other was playful and less rigid, an attitude that endeared her to the children.

The second one knew the secret that religion is more than studying theology.

Religion encompasses a spirit of excitement about the gift of life, and the promise of eternal happiness. It makes us think about ways we can be more effective in communicating the excitement that comes from experiencing God's love.

Passing on our faith is not just about communicating doctrine; it is about creating a joyful family here on earth and helping them to prepare for the joys of heaven.

The Mass is a celebration. For some it is more of a Church ritual. Those who see the Mass through the eyes of faith understand it as an act of love.

We give ourselves to God at the offertory, and God gives himself right back to us at Holy Communion.

This exchange of love is holy and produces the joyful spirit in us.

We gradually come to see that the problems of this world are monumental, but they could be infinitely worse if we forget to count our blessings each day.

Even if all the world's problems were solved tomorrow, people would still find things to complain about. Wouldn't it be a good idea if we began now to instruct our children to be more optimistic and hopeful? Let them cling to the belief that the highest values of the human spirit are attainable because of God's grace. Jesus calls us higher. We *can* teach our children to count their blessings. We *can* protect them from pessimism and fear. We *can* invite them to live a more joyful life, and best of all, we can start by helping them to see God in all the beauty they see around them.

> *Dear Lord, as the body grows and flourishes on a healthy diet, so does the soul grow and flourish on a steady diet of positive thinking. Help me to be pure of heart.*

7 Avoid Self-Sabotage

We often go against our own best interest by failing to control our thoughts. Let me give you an example of how easily a person can become disturbed.

A middle-aged woman was experiencing sharp pains in her abdomen. She went to the doctor, and he did all the tests and took X-rays. He concluded that there was nothing organically wrong with her.

When he told her this, she became enraged. She knew that the pain was not just in her imagination. Actually, he knew that too, but he could not convince her that it was in her mind. There was no infection or other physical explanation.

She went to two other doctors and got the same answers. This made her feel worse. She knew she was experiencing real pain and concluded that something must be seriously wrong. She had no idea how the mind can play tricks on us. By trusting her feelings instead of her doctors' she perpetuated her misery.

Finally she had the courage to see a psychologist. He explained that the feeling of pain was indeed real, but that her mind was deceiving her about its cause. It seems she had moved recently and was afraid of not being accepted in her new environment. This fear was a throwback to a time in her childhood when her new classmates rejected her, thus causing severe emotional distress. The hidden memory of her childhood emotional trauma triggered off the bodily aches and pains in her side.

When she finally accepted this explanation, she no longer felt she was in danger, and her pain began to dissolve.

Because this good woman did not know how to control her thoughts, she lost her objectivity and could not deal with her fears. Believe it or not there is a better way. Either we can decide to be joyful and work to eliminate toxic thinking, or we can wallow in fear and suffer its many consequences.

Joy is the enemy of fear. The Lord told us not to be afraid. When in pain, always see your doctor, of course. And never allow toxic thoughts to take over your mind.

Your body may be screaming to you to run away from some imaginary danger, but don't be fooled. Calm yourself. Take control of your thoughts. If you can't, go to a psychologist for help. Do what you have to do to remove the acute panic attack. Pray without forcing any feelings. Give yourself to God just as you are, and gradually the panic will subside.

> *Dear God, help me to spot a panic attack when it comes along, so that I may remember immediately that nervous symptoms are distressing but not dangerous.*

8 Contemplation

A young woman came to me with a spiritual problem. She said she felt like a complete failure when it came to prayer. Even though she tried and tried, she felt no love for God and had no interest in reciting prayers from a book. Prayer itself completely baffled her.

We talked for a while, and I tried to explain that when it comes to prayer you never have to force feelings of any kind. All you have to do is give yourself to God as best you can. It doesn't matter how much time you spend doing it.

I told her that one of the most beautiful prayers is the act of simply sitting quietly and enjoying the beauty of nature all around you. God is present in all of creation. One can stretch the imagination a bit and consider it as similar to experiencing God's presence in the tabernacle.

In a way, that is precisely what contemplative prayer is: awe in God's presence. No words are necessary. Contemplation is the highest form of prayer. One enters God's silence. This act of the will has nothing to do with feelings; it is simply a choice of being with the Lord.

Often God's silence will free you from the drudgery of incessant thinking, but if your mind starts racing again, ignore it and listen to the silence, which is the only language God speaks. The present moment, by the way, is the only place where the risen Lord resides.

Meeting God here and now in silence is better than engaging in vocal prayer. It quiets the mind and liberates us to relax and be with the Lord.

Pure prayer is nothing more than giving yourself to God. You stop thinking! You become silent!

The indwelling Trinity is always present. St. Paul wrote, "I live, no longer I, but Christ lives in me." Wherever one Person of the Trinity is present, all three are present. Watching a beautiful sunset, for instance, is one way to enter the presence of the Blessed Trinity. God is always in the present moment.

So minimize your use of words and simply enjoy the Lord.

No one is a failure at prayer as long as they try to relax and give themselves to God as best they can. Stop judging your prayer life and trust that the Lord will receive you into his love.

Holy Spirit, Soul of my soul, teach me how to keep it simple, so that I may enjoy you more and more.

9 Enjoy the Lord

Abbot John Chapman said, "Pure prayer is in the will to give yourself to God, when it comes to prayer you should never force feelings of any kind."

Say, "Yes, Lord, I am here, and I give myself to you, distractions and all." Pure prayer is in the will to submit to God's keeping.

The will has only one function. The will says "yes" or "no." It has nothing to do with thoughts or feelings. Even if you feel as dry as a bone or have wild distractions, it is still possible to please the Lord. Whether you are saying the Rosary or meditating, doing spiritual reading or engaging in contemplation, if you intend to give yourself to God in the process, you are praying a pure prayer.

Emotional distress, or troubling distractions do not cancel your good intentions. Whether you feel pious or sad, the desire to give yourself remains pure.

According to Father John Pierre de Caussade, the 17th-century Jesuit who authored the spiritual classic *Abandonment to Divine Providence*, "The secret of sanctity and happiness rests in one's fidelity to the will of God as it is manifested in the duty of the present moment."

The duty of the present moment could involve performing some humble task in the kitchen. It is not what you are doing that matters, it is the intention you have while doing it. Mother Teresa used to say, "It's not what you do, it's how much love you put into the doing."

You can enjoy the Lord while you brush your teeth in the morning. Instead of worrying needlessly about the future, you can enjoy the present moment with God, any time of the day.

Learn to laugh at those annoying distractions. None of us can pray as well as we think we ought to pray, but if we accept the reality of our own limitations, we will be praying as best we can, and the Lord loves us for making the effort.

We don't have to wait until we get to heaven to share in God's life of joy. Sanctifying grace gives us a share in God's happiness right now.

Lord, teach me to freshen my prayer with joy, and help me to give myself to you with a smile.

10 The Dance of Life

Not too long ago I was watching TV and came across an old movie with Fred Astaire and Ginger Rogers. The two were dressed in formal evening attire, dancing in perfect unison to the tune, "Let's Face the Music and Dance." I was captivated by their elegance and grace.

They were performing in the 1936 musical, *Follow the Fleet*. The plot is utterly forgettable, but their dance sequence has become a film classic. Fred and Ginger did the entire routine in one take, a feat unthinkable by today's standards.

The background story is simple: Fred leaves a gambling casino having lost his last dollar. Moving morosely along a river walk, he sees a beautiful young woman about to jump into the cold water below. Instinctively he leaps to save her and takes her into his arms. She is stunned as he dances her away from the dock. The music rises in the background and Fred begins to sing to her softly, "There may be troubles ahead but…let's face the music and dance."

The words of Jesus came immediately to mind as I watched them. The Lord said, "In this world you will have many troubles, but be brave for I have overcome the world" (John 16:33).

Fred and Ginger continued their magnificent ballroom dancing and her mood began to change. Finally as the music fades away, they walk off arm in arm, smiling all the way.

A miraculous healing has taken place in a few minutes, and the art form of this healing ritual was the dance itself.

It was pure Hollywood shtick, but on the other hand, it was magnificent. I saw the dance sequence as an expression of God's love in action. It was a metaphor for the Lord's saving power: Jesus Christ is ready to sweep you off your feet at a moment's notice. He will come to you when you least expect it and when you are most in need, in times of suffering and darkness. God's saving love always comes to your rescue.

We all need a savior. Our faith reassures us that God is the source of all the love the world has ever known. God inspires all the warm-hearted feelings we have ever felt. The Almighty One wants us to help one another in the dance of life by spreading the love.

Can anyone ask more of a Hollywood movie? This one was exquisite in proclaiming the saving power of love. Salvation is always near at hand.

Lord of the dance, take me into your love
and save me from the demons that haunt
me.

11 The Joy of God Is within You

A woman named Elsa was married for 20 years when she hit bottom, feeling overwhelmed with life's burdens. Her demanding husband was becoming more and more abusive and her children more and more disrespectful. She had lost her joy and didn't know how to cope. Nevertheless, as weary as she was, she managed to persevere.

Mother Teresa of Calcutta would have understood her problem very well. According to recent revelations, Mother managed to keep on caring for the poorest of the poor in spite of her emotional emptiness. How did she do it?

She simply asked the Lord to be her strength and her joy. She learned to live by faith, not by feelings. As a result, her life never stopped producing good fruit. She always depended on God's power, not her own.

Once, when she was seriously ill, she wrote, "Joy is prayer. Joy is strength. Joy is love. Joy is a net of love by which you can catch souls. God loves a cheerful giver. One gives most who gives joy. The best way to show gratitude to God and people is to accept everything with joy. Never let anything so fill you with sorrow as to make you forget the joy of the risen Christ. I tell this to my Sisters, and I tell this to you."

What an amazing insight for one who was so emotionally empty! Obviously she willed to be joyful in spite of her feelings, and she succeeded.

The famous author C.S. Lewis was not a Roman Catholic; he was an Anglican Catholic, and a strong defender of the faith. It may come as a surprise to learn that Clive Staples Lewis was, for most of his early life, a skeptic. He said it was God's grace that brought him from non-belief to Christianity.

Lewis always admired the way God's love manifested itself in the lives of holy people. He saw them risking everything to relieve the world's suffering by caring for plague victims, by defending the rights of children, and by running soup kitchens for the homeless. He saw all these activities as God's presence in our midst.

It all goes to show that the people of God, as troubled as they may be at times, can still manage to keep on keeping on. In spite of injustices, trials, and sorrows, the Lord becomes their strength and their joy. Pray for the grace to imitate the saints among us.

Lord, I beg you to be my strength and joy,
protect me from the folly of trying to do too
much on my own.

12 Faith Is a Joyful Adventure

My sister's best friend came to see me recently. She was dying of an inoperable cancer in her brain, and was understandably dejected. Before I spoke, I prayed quietly for the grace to say the right thing.

I told her that it isn't what happens to us in life that really counts, it's how we react to it. Either we allow ourselves to sink deeper into despair, or we decide to live joyfully to the end and make the most of the time remaining to us. She liked the idea and took my advice seriously.

Since then, in spite of her condition, she and her husband arranged to take a cruise to Europe on the Queen Mary II. After that they went around the country visiting their scattered children. Now, believe it or not, they are planning a trip to Tahiti.

Where did all this energy come from? She said she gives God the credit for her new attitude. Her faith in God's power, and her husband's enthusiasm to make her last days on earth a little happier, made all the difference.

Pope Benedict spoke in favor of joy and optimism at a youth rally in Cologne, Germany, at the beginning of his papacy. He said, "I would like to show them how beautiful it is to be a Christian, because the widespread idea which continues to exist is that Christianity is composed of laws and bans which one has to keep and, hence, is something toilsome and burdensome."

Putting the emphasis on joy and what we can do, rather than on what we cannot do, changes everything.

"Jesus came from the overflowing joy of God," German theologian Jürgen Moltmann writes, "and he gives up his life for the joy of the world."

"In the public ministry of Jesus," Moltmann asks, "why did he go first to the outcasts of his world, and not to the scribes and high priests?

He answers, "The inner motivation for Jesus in striking up friendships with sinners and tax collectors lies in his joy, in God's joy. Jesus does not bring a dry sympathy to us, but the inviting joy of God's kingdom to one and all."

The cross was never an end in itself. Rather, it is a prelude to Easter Sunday. Jesus said, "I have told you this so that your joy may be complete."

Life is a wonderful adventure! Don't postpone joy!

Lord, give me a share of that kind of faith and confidence. Help me to enjoy every day of my life.

13 Don't Forget to Love Yourself

How often are you inclined to put yourself down by beings too hard on yourself?

I knew a man who was overly religious. Trying so hard to be a saint, he became inordinately critical of himself. This led to mental health problems. He was basically a good man, but he always found a way to focus on the things he disliked about himself. So sad!

I told him that Jesus told us to love ourselves. Jesus said, "Love God with your whole heart, and love your neighbor *as you love yourself.*" This verse is a key text in the Old Testament as well. In fact, it is the Supreme Law, a divine command to love oneself. Those who do not know how to become their own best friend are guilty of a form of "stinking" thinking.

Why not choose to be happy? Have a more positive mind-set, and decide to take God's command to love yourself more seriously.

When alcoholics and drug addicts enter rehab they believe that with the help of God they can develop a good attitude, and allow the Lord to help them recover from their addiction.

If they can recover, so can all of us. With God's help, all things are possible. Don't let the past drag us down. Become your own best friend.

Here are some things to think about as you embark on this noble task:

You are not your thoughts; rather, you are the observer of your thoughts.

Reject troubling thoughts. Stop living inside your own head.

Replace bad thoughts with the living experiences of one of your five senses. Practice living in the present moment. Smell the roses, breathe the fresh air, watch the birds, taste your favorite dessert. The Lord is only to be found in the present moment. Ask for your daily bread. He promised to refresh those who come to him with their troubles. He is in the here and now. Call on the name of Jesus.

You have the power to choose your thoughts. Once you decide to live in the present and feel the wind on your face, it will reduce your symptoms of fear and anxiety. Enjoy your precious life with God now. Love yourself, body and soul.

Dear Holy Spirit, Soul of my soul, protect me, and bring me into your presence. Cleanse me of my toxic thoughts, and let me be with you in your joy.

14 Jesus Is the Source of Our Joy

I know a woman who was baptized recently. It was a big day in her life when she accepted Jesus as Lord. Being Jewish, she had an abhorrence of turning away from her heritage, but once she came to see Jesus as the true Messiah of her Hebrew heritage she realized that she was happy to be where she felt God wanted her to be. Her journey of faith brought her to a newfound joy.

Everyone is free to accept or reject Jesus. Accepting him is a matter of faith. Christians through the ages have learned that Jesus has the power to open our hearts to a joy that this world cannot give.

The question most people ask is this: How can I find this joy; how can I experience supernatural joy in my own life? The answer is that you can, if you have the faith.

There are two kinds of faith: natural and supernatural. We live by natural faith every day when we believe in the reliability of maps and weather forecasts. Even though we don't know the mapmakers or the weather reporters personally, we put our "natural" faith in them. Supernatural faith gives us the ability to trust Jesus Christ. He is the Anointed One who came to bring God into our world. St. Paul describes God as: Peace, Love, and Joy.

In the New Testament for instance, Jesus reveals God to us as a merciful Father. A believer takes Jesus at his word and knows he is telling us the truth. Believing in the authority of Jesus makes all the difference.

We learn about our purpose in life and our future destiny in heaven from the Bible, which is not merely a collection of books and theological opinions, it is a spiritual treasure trove of divine revelation and ancient wisdom. The Bible teaches us who we are, why we are here, and where we are going.

The Bible teaches us that Jesus fulfilled the ancient Messianic prophecies, and that he claimed divine authority over the Law and the Sabbath. Jesus is the magnificent centerpiece of the entire Bible, both Old and New Testaments; he is the Lord of life.

Almighty Father, thank you for sending Jesus.
I humbly offer my gratitude for all your
magnificent gifts.

15 Joy Out of Sorrow

My mother suffered for seven years before her death. She had a combination of painful ailments ranging from severe asthma, to rheumatoid arthritis, to a painful colon condition, which took three surgeries to correct. She finally succumbed out of sheer exhaustion in 1957, three years before my ordination.

I found it remarkable how she managed to be brave through it all. She remained calm and was an inspiration to the whole family.

Here are some of the lessons I learned from watching my mother try to cope with pain as she wasted away:

- Unavoidable suffering is debilitating, unbearable, and frightening. A person should take whatever medication is needed to ease the discomfort. Carrying on with dignity is not always possible without God's grace, therefore praying for that grace is an important part of coping. God does answer all our prayers.
- Uniting your suffering to the pain of Jesus on the cross will give your suffering meaning. Offering it for your own salvation and for the salvation of others can give an enriched meaning to your life.
- Pain, in and of itself, is an evil thing, but when it is accepted and offered to the Lord, it becomes an intimate way of sharing Jesus' burden on the cross.

It is a mysterious way of participating in the Lord's redemption of the world. This thought often turns healthy people off, but when you are dying, it is suddenly emblazoned with meaning and becomes a wonderful comfort.

- Praying for a happy, pain-free death is a good thing at any stage in life. It is also wise to pray in advance for the wisdom and courage to bear any crosses that life might send you in the future. Trusting the future to God's providence is the way to overcome needless fear.
- It is all right to beg to be liberated from pain, Jesus himself did that: "Father, if it be possible, take this cup from me, but not my will but thine be done."
- The sick patient who believes in the Lord knows that heaven is as close as next summer's vacation, and maybe closer. All will be well.
- Joy is not a feeling; it is an attitude. Joy is possible not only in good times, but also in times of suffering. The human body carries the pain, but the spirit is the custodian of Divine Joy. Body and soul coexist in this way all through life, and even more so at the end. The fullness of joy is the ultimate reward of a life surrendered to God.

Dear Lord, deliver me from the fear of death,
and in times of pain help me to know that
joy that this world cannot give.

16 The Joy of Forgiveness

Tom, a retired law enforcement officer, felt he was cheated when he stepped down from his job at age 50. After 30 years of service he was denied the promotion and raise he felt he deserved. The bitterness and hurt he experienced lingered in his brain for many years after that. He simply could not get rid of his resentment.

He was a good Catholic man in every other respect, but he harbored unforgiving and angry thoughts. He never seemed to understand that Jesus wants us to forgive others more for our own good than for theirs.

The German mystic Meister Eckhart wrote, "None of you has a spirit so heavy, nor an intelligence so feeble; none of you is so far from God that you lack the ability to find Joy in Him."

We don't even realize that by holding on to resentments, we harbor an unforgiving heart. "Forgive us our trespasses as we forgive those who trespass against us." These are difficult words. The Lord's Prayer is not easy to live by. It tells us to let go of the unforgiving spirit, and say yes to God, "forgive seventy times seven."

Angry feelings shut out joy. Even when there has been an injustice, it is in our own self interest to let go of resentment. A great injustice may have occurred, but should we allow it to drag us down forever? If you can't forget the bad things that happen to you, at least pray for the grace to forgive. And say a prayer for the one who offended you. Do that as often as your anger returns. To forgive is divine.

Jesus forgave his tormentors while he was hanging on the cross. He even made excuses for them: "Forgive them Father, they know not what they are doing" (Luke 23:34).

We "fore-give" before we feel like it. We forgive now, not because the person deserves it, but because the Lord asks it of us. Every time you pray for the person, you are telling the Lord that you want to be a true Christian.

Forgiveness is in the will, not the feelings. Forgive, and your peace and joy will gradually return. "A cheerful glance brings joy to the heart" (Proverbs 15:30).

Dearest Jesus, I want with all my heart to forgive and forget. Help me to find strength to do as You ask.

17 Learn to Forgive Yourself

Millions of brokenhearted people live their lives in quiet desperation feeling guilty. One elderly woman had an abortion in her youth, and she never got over it. She was still punishing herself, years later, believing that God was going to punish her.

She had confessed her sin many years before, but still acted as though God never heard that confession and never forgave her.

People forget that the greatest sins ever committed on earth in no way put a limit on God's infinite mercy. There is no need to perpetuate feelings of guilt, no need to keep on punishing oneself. The best thing is to thank God for his mercy, and then move on with life.

Feelings follow thoughts. If you fail to accept God's love and forgiveness, you set yourself up as one who refuses to honor God's love. We cannot allow ourselves to be too proud to accept God's mercy and love. The guilt feelings will only subside when we are humble enough to trust in God's power to bring good out of evil.

God always forgives those who ask. "Forgive them Father, for they know not what they are doing." The message of God's mercy may seem too good to be true. But if we accept God's forgiveness, the gift of peace will come to us.

Acceptance purifies the soul and brings relief to the wounded spirit. "The forgiven penitent," said Pope John Paul II, "is reconciled with himself in his inmost being, where he regains his own true identity."

Very often those who cling to guilty feelings are putting themselves above God's mercy. They believe that they are unworthy of forgiveness, so they punish themselves endlessly in order to become worthy. Jesus said, "Do not be afraid… your sins are forgiven." Take him at his word.

The penitent needs to bow in gratitude, not fear. Thank Jesus for his forgiveness. Peaceful feelings will follow eventually. Forgive yourself now. If you can't seem to be able to do it, at least ask for the grace to forgive yourself, and be patient.

Forgiveness is in the will, and the will has only one function. The will says yes or no. Say yes to God and forgive yourself. Do it because of the knowledge of God's love. He wants you to share in his peace and joy. Change your thinking pattern and be at peace.

Dear Jesus, teach me to be still; teach me to accept your love and forgiveness. I know you are blessing me every moment of my life, and I thank you with all my heart.

18 Holiness Is Possible

Holiness is not the reward of a lifetime of loving service. We give a lifetime of loving service because we are holy. Holiness is not the reward of great generosity. We are generous because we are holy.

Holiness is essentially the sincere desire to accept God's will in all things.

This acceptance is the goal of a healthy spiritual life. To attain any degree of holiness we have to make a commitment to do God's will, as we understand it. This implies a willingness to accept the bad things that God permits to happen in our lives.

Bad things always happen to good people. For instance, by standing up for truth and justice you will certainly attract opponents. There is an abundance of misery and injustice in the world. Acceptance of God's will doesn't mean that we should become doormats or cowards.

It's normal to react with anger in the face of sin or injustice. Jesus did that when he turned over the tables of the moneychangers in the Temple. Many of the saints fell into emotional turmoil as they tried to carry out God's will in this world. There will always be painful times.

The constant effort to accept God's will can bring with it unavoidable conflict. Sacrifices made in the name of justice are sure signs of holiness.

We offer up our suffering with Jesus Christ on the cross. He was the innocent victim of the most outrageous injustice. The servant cannot be greater than the master.

The late Father Thomas Merton, a Trappist monk, wrote about his inner turmoil and offered this humble prayer:

> *My Lord God, I have no idea where I am going. I do not see the road ahead of me. I cannot know for certain where it will end. Nor do I really know myself. The fact that I think I am following your will does not mean that I am actually doing so. But I believe the desire to please you actually does in fact please you. And I hope that I have that desire in all that I am doing. I hope that I will never do anything apart from that desire. And I know that if I do that, you will lead me by the right road. Though I may seem lost and in the shadow of death, I will not fear, for you are ever with me, and you will never leave me to face my perils alone.*

19 Are You There, God?

"I like your articles," a woman said, "but there is still something nagging at me. Why is it so hard for me to connect with my ever-loving, Supreme Being?"

St. Augustine answered this question centuries ago: "Our hearts are restless until they rest in Thee O Lord." The feeling of dissatisfaction is universal. Maybe God just wants us to keep on searching.

Pope Benedict XVI speaks of this inner longing in his book *Jesus of Nazareth*: "It belongs to [our] nature that [we want to] stand face-to-face with God....We will come to see God when we enter into 'the mind of Christ.'"

How do we do that? St. Paul said, in Galatians 2:20, "It is no longer I who live, but it is Christ who lives in me." In other words, we have to change. Jesus Christ is the revelation of God. We have to turn to him.

"Though he was in the form of God, he did not regard equality with God as something to be exploited, but emptied himself, taking the form of a slave, being born in human likeness" (Philippians 2:6-7).

Good people from the beginning of time have done everything from sacrificing their young to enduring long fasts in order to connect with their Creator. We know that when you love someone, and they love you, there is a great desire for union. We long for the experience of a noble love relationship.

Correspondingly, we long for an emotional connection with God. However, in the realm of the supernatural, we need to do it God's way. We are called to turn to Jesus and deepen our trust in him. He is God incarnate.

Occasionally some of us are lifted up to mystical heights, but only rarely. More often than not, our prayers remain dry. Still, there can be a subtle joy in the knowledge that we are loved and never alone.

It is possible to freshen your prayer with joy when you believe deeply in the love of Christ. Ignore the negative feelings. You can minimize the importance of your feelings of loneliness by rejecting those negative thoughts that undermine your confidence in God's love.

Jesus said, "I am the resurrection and the life. Those who believe in me will live, and even though they die, will live, and everyone who lives and believes in Me will never die" (John 11:25-26).

Lord, help me to make the leap of faith that will bring me nearer to you. At least help me to be content with my natural state of discontent.

20 Believing in God's Love

An elderly nun, after years of dedication and prayer, felt that she had made no progress at all from the time she was a young novice. Why? Because spiritually, she felt as dry as a bone.

She certainly believed in God's love, but she couldn't feel it.

Trusting Jesus is obviously an act of the will, not a feeling.

Look to Jesus, and try to figure it out for yourself. He was condemned as a heretic, and yet he went on. He was viciously ridiculed and attacked by the elders, and yet he went on. He was plotted against, condemned, and vilified, and yet he went on. Finally he was arrested, beaten, and crucified, and on the cross he said, "My God why hast thou abandoned me?"

Through it all he knew he was loved, his trust never wavered, but he certainly didn't have an easy time of it. Should this information be of any help to the dejected nun? I think so. I think she focused too much on her weakness, and not enough on all the good she did in her life.

The most joyful utterance Jesus ever expressed was on the cross: "It is consummated." At last the pain of life had come to an end, and he had accomplished his mission. In this world we will never find the paradise we long for.

We are at our best when our lives are an imitation of the life of Christ.

I would encourage anyone who is experiencing dryness at prayer not to be afraid. You may not be praying as well as you would like to pray or as well as you have prayed in the past, but you are probably praying as best you can. Abbot John Chapman said that there is a certain peace that comes from knowing that if the Lord wanted you to be lifted higher, he would do that for you. So presume it is his will for you to suffer dryness when you long for ecstasy.

By offering all your sufferings and humiliations to the Lord, you are sharing in his suffering and death, his universal act of redemption, saving souls, liberating captives, and gaining heaven. There is a deep level of joy in knowing this.

Be content if your prayer is flagging; it really doesn't matter.

Dear Jesus, help me to freshen my prayer with joy and acceptance.

21 A Joy Not of This World

The early Christian martyrs sang songs of joy before they were led to the lions. They faced their sufferings with dignity because they had a deep knowledge of God's love. This awareness of being favored by God filled the saints with joy. It goes entirely against the grain of common sense, but it is true nevertheless.

Mary the Mother of Jesus stood by the cross. Can anyone imagine the depth of her sorrow? And yet she said, "My spirit finds joy in God, my Savior (Luke 1:47).

How can joy and sorrow coexist in one person?

Spiritual joy does flourish in the midst of sorrow. It baffles the mind, but it happens nevertheless. Spiritual joy delights the soul even in the midst of trials and persecution.

A prisoner may take a beating, withholding secret information that would mean the certain death of his companions. Inwardly he rejoices in not giving up his secret. He is saving lives.

Spiritual joy comes from faith in the knowledge that we can return love to the God who loves us. We believe that we are no longer poor, helpless creatures left defenseless in a brutal world. Rather, we are children of a loving Father who is protecting us. We are strong with his strength, and therefore joyful because, "In him we live and breathe and have our being."

The foundation of our joy is in the knowledge of our blessedness.

Jesus said, "Blessed are they who are persecuted for the sake of righteousness, for theirs is the Kingdom of Heaven" (Matthew 5:10). All the Beatitudes are simply different ways of presenting the same idea; namely, that spiritual joy comes to those who really believe that they are loved.

To be loved is to be favored. In spite of any negative feelings to the contrary, our faith teaches us that the favor of the Lord rests upon us, not because of our worthiness, but because of God's wonderful generosity.

This knowledge enables us to trust the Lord when he tells us "be not afraid." Relief comes to the soul when we shed our fears. This new state of being enables joy to flood the soul. A fearless soul soars to new heights.

Dear Lord, help me to experience the joy that this world cannot give.

22 Joy Is the Fruit of Faith

Joy is not merely a matter of feelings. Joy is the by-product of a strong faith in God's love. Joy is also the by-product of a meaningful life.

Studying for many years in school can be a drag, but it all leads to a wonderful graduation ceremony. The whole process is part of the joy of accomplishment. Perhaps the preparation is painful at times, but it is always full of hope. Feelings may flag, but the will sets the goal.

The spiritual challenge of joy requires long-term planning and requires an ability to deal with your fears. For instance, the fear of failing can keep a person from actually entering college in the first place.

The Bible continually tells us, "Do not be afraid," but many of us haven't understood that we have the power to overcome fear. These words of wisdom come directly from God, and they have to be taken seriously. If you act against your fears you will become a much happier person.

All you need to do is believe in the truth that God is unchanging love. Feelings can be of help once you have the faith, but more often than not they lead you astray.

Here is the theological foundation of a strong spiritual life: "God so loved the world that he gave his only son… so that the world might be saved through him" (John 3:16-17).

Jesus spoke these words to reveal the mystery of God's love. He came to bring joy and liberation. He came to unite us to the Father, who possesses the fullness of joy. Fear is the enemy of joy; therefore, God wants us to banish unreasonable fear from our lives.

There are always some legitimate worries that we can never get rid of, but needless fear needs to be banished.

When Pope John Paul II said that "Christ came to bring joy, joy to children, joy to parents, joy to students, joy to teachers, joy to friends and families, and joy to the sick and elderly," he was telling us not to be afraid, either of God, or of the world around us. With God on our side, who can be against us? All things are possible.

Franklin D. Roosevelt put it this way; The only thing to fear, is fear itself. Truer words were never spoken. To overcome your fears, turn immediately to the Lord. With God's help you are never left alone without protection.

Prayer will put you in touch with God's power, and he will do for you what you cannot yet do for yourself!

Dear Lord, take my fears away and give me the confidence I need to carry on with joy and courage.

23 Be Yourself

Unless you find your purpose in life, you will never feel fulfilled.

The Buddhists have the law of Dharma, which claims that there is only one sin; namely, to walk away from your true purpose.

All through my college years I had a secret interest in the priesthood. However, I was convinced I didn't have a vocation. It was too much for me. Quite frankly, I was afraid of failing.

What I didn't realize was that my whole being was yearning to be a priest. I never heard any voice calling me, but down deep I had this desire I couldn't dismiss. I began to believe that being a priest was what God wanted me to do with my life.

Once I decided, a great peace came over me and I never looked back. I finally felt that I had found my true self. This enabled me to live in God's joy, in a way I had never experienced before.

We all come from God, and we are meant to rest in God. In some incomprehensible way, God, without taking our freedom away, is directing us to overcome fear and follow our dream. This implies that our union with God depends more on God's love for us than on our love for God.

No matter what decision we make about our future, God will be there blessing us, but the ideal is to get in touch with our secret desires and trust God's love to support us. We gradually become confident about following the difficult paths set before us. We have the courage to take risks, knowing that God's strength will enable us to transcend our human limitations.

For instance, your heart may be heavy and full of fear. Instead of letting that fear defeat you, use it as a stepping-stone to greater freedom. Don't let any fear drag you down. Give it to God, and trust the future to divine providence.

God will take care of all the fears that threaten you. Enjoy each day as a unique gift and a new beginning. God wants us to be happy right now. Live in the present moment. Choose to be a saint.

St. Teresa of Avila always repeated this prayer: "Let nothing disturb you, let nothing cause you fear. Patience obtains all. God is unchanging love. God alone suffices."

Dear Lord, help me to be my true self by trusting you completely.

24 How to Spot a Friend

Always act according to your convictions, said my late friend Father James McCoy, S.J. He was on the faculty at Fordham University when I was a student there. Father Jim was a kind man, but he always followed his own counsel. Jim was an independent thinker and a man of great strength and determination. He had one of the sharpest minds I have ever encountered.

He was a pillar of strength for me when I was floundering as a young college student. Later in life Jim became my spiritual director. His sage advice helped me immensely over the years.

Never once did he suggest that I become a priest. He would brush off my attempts to discuss it, saying that it was an issue between God and me. In fact, he even went so far as to say that I was probably mistaking a general vocation to holiness for a vocation to the priesthood. This let me off the hook and comforted me.

At the time, I didn't really want to make the commitment. Believing that I was only called to holiness and not the priesthood gave me a temporary excuse to stall—but not for long. Eventually I surrendered to that inner yearning, and once I accepted my inner voice as a true calling, I was at peace. Jim was then delighted that I had made the decision on my own, without any pressure from him or anyone else.

One of the things I admired about Father Jim was that he had absolutely no interest in money or material things. He was genuinely poor in spirit. He was as comfortable in the homes of wealthy families as he was talking to the homeless. He will probably never be canonized, but he was a saint as far as I'm concerned.

How does one spot a good friend? A good friend listens. A good friend sets a noble example. A good friend encourages, without taking your freedom away. A good friend is there when you need to talk. A good friend helps you, but lets you find your own way.

Dear Lord, help me to find a good friend and to be a good friend.

25 Abiding in God's Love

Everyone gets discouraged at times, feeling that there is so much to do and so little time to do it. St. Augustine said, "Do what you can, and pray for what you cannot yet do." In the meantime, keep abiding in the Lord. The Lord will heal all our wounds and forgive all our misdeeds. All we have to do is try to abide in him.

"Abide in me," Jesus said. "In this world you will have many troubles, but do not be afraid for I have overcome the world."

It is a wonderful experience to abide in God's presence. Even when our thoughts are a million miles away from God most of the day, we can still sense divine presence within our soul.

Here's a little prayer that I like to say to renew my morning offering:

"Holy Spirit, Soul of my soul, I adore you…thank you for loving me. Guide and protect me; help me to reverence you living in me, and teach me to be responsive to the needs of others." Repeating this prayer often helps to remind me that I am a carrier of divine love and joy.

Recently I gave a day of recollection on joy and was asked to define spiritual joy. "Spiritual joy is the act of consciously abiding in God's unchanging love," I answered, "and it requires a leap of faith." The sense of

God brings joy to the souls of those who deeply believe in his love.

There are two kinds of joy. There is natural joy, like holding a happy baby, and there is supernatural joy, which comes from one's faith in the knowledge of God's loving presence. This is a joy that this world cannot give.

Julian of Norwich said, "The greatest honor you can give to Almighty God, greater than all your penances and sacrifices, is to live gladly, joyfully because of the knowledge of his love."

Even a sinner who is caught up in some situation not of his or her liking can abide in God's love. The holy desire to be a saint is the beginning of sanctity. As the new Catechism puts it, the inner readiness to be more receptive to the hidden truth that the Lord is in our midst, is already an opening to conversion; healing has already begun.

Dear Lord, help us to believe.

26 Tell a Loved One You Care

The happiest moment of my life was the day of my ordination, May 28, 1960. My dear mother had died three years earlier, but, thankfully, my dad was there to share the joy. As he came forward for my first priestly blessing I could see that he was weeping a bit; I know I was. The moment had come at last. After all those years of study and preparation, I was finally an ordained priest of Jesus Christ.

Afterward, we all went out for a meal to celebrate the joyous event. My dad was thrilled to be the host of the party. I'm sure he said some touching things to me. It wasn't until 25 years later, however, that he wrote me a note to share his feelings about that day:

"Dear Son, Congratulations on your Silver Jubilee. I never told you this before, but the fondest and happiest moment of my life was the day you were ordained, and I went up to get your first blessing. I was so emotionally charged that as I returned up the aisle, I couldn't see where I was going. I just dropped into a vacant pew, buried my head, and had a good cry. They were happy tears, even though my one regret was that mother did not live long enough to share this joy with us. But I'm sure she enjoyed watching over us from heaven. Keep up the good work, and pray for me always. I am happy to say that I am your father. With a heart full of love, Dad."

My eyes become a little teary when I read that note. Of all the honors and awards I've received in life, nothing compares with that communication from my father. It recaptured a special memory that I will always treasure. My dad died in 1992, at the age of 85.

Never underestimate the impact that a simple note to a loved one can have on them. Any attempt to express your deepest feelings will carry a lot of weight.

Why not think of someone you can share some noble thought with today. Someone dear to you will be especially grateful. A loving note might be just the thing they need right now to help them through a difficult time. Give someone the boost that only you can give.

Dear Lord, Giver of all good gifts, thank you for all the love I have received in my life.

27 How to Celebrate 75 Years

On September 8, 2006 I turned 75. Looking back I can remember my father's 75th birthday. He and his contemporaries were all slowly falling apart, but they didn't seem to notice. They couldn't believe they were approaching 80, and that's exactly the way I feel right now.

Even though I'm in the sunset of my life, I still look forward to many more years. While enjoying the moment, I know that one day I will die; we all will. I don't dread the thought of it. Jesus said, "Do not be afraid," and I take him at his word.

Except for my arthritic knees, I find life exhilarating, and I am especially grateful for the gift of faith. More importantly I am in love with joy. I sense God's presence in all the beauty of the world. I am surrounded by love.

Nevertheless, my body keeps sending warning signals. I had radical prostate surgery for cancer in 2002, and managed to survive. My cataracts have been removed, and some of my teeth have been replaced. My sense of humor, however, is still in good shape.

I realize that the miracle of God is there to behold at every sunrise. Every time I get up to greet the day I am filled with gratitude. I feel as though something wonderful is going to happen, but I don't know exactly what or when. I hope to live to be a hundred, but reading the obituaries, I see that many people, a lot younger than I, have passed on. Everyone my age knows that graduation day can't be far away.

Last week I was in agony with a toothache. The tooth was extracted and afterward I felt great relief. I am not recommending a tooth extraction as a way of finding nirvana. I simply wanted to mention it to make the point that we have to keep our bodily aches and pains in perspective.

The pains of this world are passing, whereas the joys of the soul are ongoing. We reap what we sow. Those who choose to be joyful, even in the midst of setbacks, are in a better position to follow St. Paul, who said, "Rejoice always!"

That may be hard to do, but with God's grace, it's not impossible.

Once again, I offer this quote of Blessed Julian of Norwich: "The greatest honor we can give to Almighty God is to live joyfully because of the knowledge of his love."

Dear Lord, help me to decide to be happy,
lead me to your joy day by day.

28 The Passion of Jesus

Mother Teresa of Calcutta encouraged her followers to radiate joy. She managed to do this even when she experienced personal distress:

"To be really united to Jesus we must all strive to be united with him in his Passion. It is his Passion to be intensely aware of the suffering of others. He unites with the suffering of the poorest of the poor and wants to help them. He wants to bring his love, peace, and joy to them, and he needs us to do that. And that is why we must radiate joy!"

Suffering and joy are not mutually exclusive ideas. I found Mother's emphasis on joy intriguing. She spoke of Christ's Passion as "a yearning to help those in need." Most of us think of the Passion of Christ in terms of his physical suffering. She saw it on a deeper level.

The cross was never intended to be an end in itself. The cross is a prelude to Easter. The Passion of Christ was something that was part of his entire life, since he always went out of his way to help the downtrodden. For doing this he was called a troublemaker.

His Passion and death were the direct result of his passion for the poor. Jesus told the outcasts that they were not cursed. They had come to believe they were because of the false teaching of the Pharisees. Jesus told them that they were blessed. The Eight Beatitudes were a reproach to the Pharisees, who, not surprisingly, became infuriated with him.

According to Mother Teresa, being united in spirit with Jesus not only means offering up your suffering with his, but entering fully into his passion to help the most marginalized of society.

Our physical suffering, when offered in union with the pain of Christ on the cross, is redemptive. It purifies the soul and wins us grace. But a fuller participation in his life is possible when we become as passionate as he was in helping the poorest of the poor.

Pain becomes holy when it is united with the pain of Christ. Therefore the sacrifices we make in the name of love do not diminish us. Rather they bring us joy, which is the by-product of love.

Let us bring "joy to the world," as Jesus did, by helping others to rise above their plight.

Dear Jesus, teach me how to bring your healing to the world.

29 You Are Blessed

It's amazing how a grateful heart can clear away the cobwebs of sadness, doubt, suspicion, and disappointment. Once you count your blessings, you will begin to develop an attitude of joy that will stay with you and lighten your burden. Getting through the disappointments of life may take some planning.

There will always be frustrations and disappointments, but each day can also bring moments of joy. In her book *War Within and Without*, Anne Lindbergh tells how she dealt with times when her joy seemed to evaporate. She resolved to think about the moments of satisfaction that came her way each day; moments of laughter and kindness provided by her family and friends. "Every day has these moments of pure joy," she told herself, "even on the dullest and saddest day."

When we make a point of appreciating the little daily joys of life, we can begin to relax more, and take pleasure in them. Some blessings are so subtle we can easily miss them if we are not watchful; like the memory of a special smile, or a beautiful flower in full bloom, or a welcome letter from a friend. All the little joys of life can contribute to a brighter mood.

The experiences that lift the spirit can be savored for days, and the list is limitless. Some people make a deliberate decision to count their blessings, and they keep a gratitude journal to sharpen their skill at it.

Think of the love you've received, not the hate.
Think of the smiles you've seen, not the frowns.
Think of the praise you've been given, not the hurts.
Think of the good you've done, not the bad.
Think of the prayers you've offered, not the distractions.
Think of God's forgiveness, not your guilt.
Think of the laughter, not the tears.

AUTHOR UNKNOWN

Offer all your joys, and even your sorrows to the Lord with heartfelt thanks. This applies to the great losses we have to endure. If you're grieving because someone you love has died or gone away, thank the Lord for all the wonderful years you had with the person you miss so much. Shift the focus a bit, and be grateful.

Being alive is the greatest of all of God's gifts. You may not appreciate it fully right now, but being human means that you are going to live in God's joy for all eternity. You and your loved ones are immortal beings. You will be able to enjoy your precious life both now and forever.

You are indeed blessed; too blessed to be stressed.

Heavenly Father, purify my good intentions and help me to bear rich and abundant good fruit for your honor and glory.

30 Be a Messenger of Joy

St. Francis of Assisi once wrote, “For what else are the servants of God but his minstrels, whose work is to lift people’s hearts and move them to spiritual gladness?”

As we come to the end of this little book, I pray that I can lift your spirit a little bit so that you will aspire to new heights of gladness.

The simple wisdom of St. Francis is that we are all called to be instruments of God’s joy to the world. This is an idea worthy of deep reflection.

Our mission as Christians is to carry God’s love and joy into daily life. St. Francis lived to bring God to those most in need, especially the poor. Why are we so blind to the plight of the poor, the sick, and the lonely? They remain in isolation, without a visitor or a sign of love.

This apathy to the needs of others is something of an epidemic, which makes the words of St. Francis so much more compelling. He challenges us to bring the love and joy of God “to lift people’s hearts, and move them to spiritual gladness.”

We get so many ecclesiastical documents and parish bulletins that allude to this mission to carry the love and joy of God into the fray of everyday life, but it often falls off the radar screen in terms of our priorities.

There are sick people who need to be visited, oppressed people who need to be uplifted, and lonely people who need to be consoled, and we have the ability to offer love, solace, and hope. Cheerful acquiescence in the will of God is the ideal. St. Francis called it, "spiritual gladness." To be minstrels of the Lord is a joyful ministry. You will get more out of it than you give.

Oddly enough, the works of mercy bring an abundance of joy to those who perform them. Ministers of joy always tell us that they have never been as happy as when they get out of themselves for a few hours a week.

So many do not feel that they have any mission in life. But that is simply not true. The mission is there for those who have eyes to see. Every soul, including yours, contains the seeds of love. Spread them generously around your local world, and enjoy your precious life.

Dearest Jesus, take away my apathetic spirit and make me holy.